PROMETHEAN ACTION

On X @PrometheanActn
www.PrometheanAction.com
Rumble.com/c/PrometheanAction
Facebook.com/PrometheanAction

A PATH TO VICTORY AND PROSPERITY
FOR ALL THE AMERICAN PEOPLE

What President Trump Can Do With the American System 2.0

Table of Contents

Introduction	2
Part 1 — The Founding of the American System: Alexander Hamilton & Public Credit	4
Part 2 — Science of Negentropic Economic Growth: The American System 2.0	10
Part 3 — On The Significance of Space and Fusion: Mankind's True Place in the Universe	28

Written by: Benjamin Deniston, Robert Ingraham

Contributors: Michael Carr, Brian Lantz, Michael Steger, Kevin Zondervan

COPYRIGHT © OCTOBER 2024 PROMETHEAN ACTION, ALL RIGHTS RESERVED.

Cover design by Adam Sturman (photo credit: Official White House Photo by Shealah Craighead). Layout by Benjamin Deniston.

Introduction

What you are reading is a document which we at Promethean Action urge you to study and circulate as widely as possible. A free version of this pamphlet is available on the Promethean Action website. It can be printed or emailed to friends, colleagues, and activists. Links to it can be posted on X and other social media platforms. We believe the ideas contained in this pamphlet are critical to rallying the American people around a policy for a second Trump administration which will create a productive, prosperous and happy future for all Americans long into the future.

*In brief, Promethean Action is building a coalition of Americans for the revival and advancement of the "American System of Economics" which was used to build our great nation: **a coalition for the American System 2.0**. Will you become part of that coalition?*

President Trump and the MAGA movement are absolutely on the right track. For two years, President Trump has been outlining key policies under the banner of Agenda47, and the 2024 GOP Platform is excellent. The Platform includes a dedication to "the Forgotten Men and Women of America," and opens with an emphasis on production and energy.

> Common Sense tells us clearly that if we don't have Domestic Manufacturing with low inflation, not only will our Economy—and even our Military Equipment and Supplies—be at the mercy of Foreign Nations, but our Towns, Communities, and People cannot thrive. The Republican Party must return to its roots as the Party of Industry, Manufacturing, Infrastructure, and Workers. President Trump's economic policy to end Inflation and return Manufacturing Jobs is not only what the American Economy and American Workers need right now, it is also what they want right now... Common Sense tells us clearly that we must unleash American Energy if we want to destroy Inflation and rapidly bring down prices, build the Greatest Economy in History, revive our Defense Industrial Base, fuel Emerging Industries, and establish the United States as the Manufacturing Superpower of the World.

As with many of our greatest presidents in the past (from John Quincy Adam to Abraham Lincoln, William McKinley, Franklin Roosevelt, and John F. Kennedy), President Trump and many involved in the MAGA movement have been looking back to the principles and policies of the American System. This is clearly reflected in Trump's economic plan, which centers around the following objectives:

- Becoming a manufacturing superpower
- Reduce regulations
- Lower taxes
- Institute fair trade, using tariffs as required
- Become world's dominant energy producer
- Champion innovation

This is the right approach, but it can and must be taken further. While President Trump's first term provided a desperately needed four-year period of growth, the American economy has been in decline for 50 years (since the early 1970s, when we replaced American System policies with the insanities of a post-industrial economy, globalization, and radical environmentalism), and reversing two generations of degradation will be no small feat. What we're providing to you here is the key to not only securing another four years of economic growth, but ensuring that that is just the beginning of a new era of prosperity.

As we present in the conclusion of this pamphlet, the secret to why the American System works goes beyond formulaic policy frameworks, and into the most fundamental issues of mankind's place in the universe. Corrupted scientific and educational institutions have attempted to demoralize our citizens with the false claim that mankind is insignificant in the universe. Elites have pushed a degenerate culture that degrades the image of man. The success of the American System 2.0 depends upon embracing a renewed image of man as a positive creative force.

What Follows Below

The first section of this document provides an overview of core aspects of the original American System of economics which have not yet been adequately taken up by the MAGA movement: *public credit and national banking, as rooted in Treasury Secretary Alexander Hamilton's original policies.*

The second section introduces the groundbreaking work of American physical economist Lyndon LaRouche. There, we show how LaRouche's discoveries in physical economics provide the foundations for what we can now call the American System 2.0, rooted in a new scientific understanding of negentropic growth in economies. From this standpoint, we show how to approach manufacturing policies and infrastructure projects to ensure they generate the most value and negentropic growth over the next generation.

The third section addresses the profound and little-understood scientific and cultural issues at the core. Mankind is a force for good in the universe, not a virus, as the radical environmentalists say. As with the Golden Renaissance in 15th century Europe, today we must again embrace and celebrate the beauty of mankind. We must show children the true meaning of their lives, by giving them the opportunity to participate in creating a better future for their family, community, and country, ensuring every citizen has the right to participate in economic progress as an immortal creative action. Nothing more clearly represents that today than the coming colonization of space, as the development of an interplanetary economy is the coming next chapter in the long book of human history.

We find ourselves today, not only in a moment of great crisis, but also at a moment of great opportunity. Perhaps our most important objective is to provide hope and optimism to the American people by demonstrating how we can unleash the greatest economic revolution in human history and create an American culture of optimism, celebrating the beauty of mankind and human progress. This can be done, and the time to act is now. We're asking you to not only read and understand this material, but to get involved, and help ensure we make this a reality.

Join our campaign for the American System 2.0

Prom.ac/AmSys2

Promethean Action is building a political alliance amongst our nation's producers.

We're looking for people involved in technology, manufacturing, science, construction, and any other productive enterprise, who can help craft and implement the greatest economic program in our nation's history.

Follow the link to let us know how you can help!

Part 1 — The Founding of the American System

Alexander Hamilton & Public Credit

Today, we are confronted with the challenge of practically rebuilding the American physical economy from the ground up. It is a monumental endeavor. America's productive economic power has been decimated over the last 50 years, and tens of millions of so-called deplorable American citizens have been declared useless eaters by our political and financial elite.

Going back to 2016, then presidential candidate Trump and other MAGA leaders began referencing the American System by name and/or advocating core American System policies, such as tariffs designed to protect domestic production. While this alone is a major breakthrough, more emphasis needs to be placed on American System policies of national banking and public credit, as originally conceived by our first Treasury Secretary Alexander Hamilton. Between 1790 and 1795, Hamilton authored six works on economic policy. Today, no one should be allowed to have any influence over economic and banking policy unless he or she has studied the two most important of those reports: *The Report on a National Bank* (December, 1790) and *The Report on the Subject of Manufactures* (December, 1791).

Alexander Hamilton (1789-1795). Painting (1806) John Trumbull.

What Hamilton established was a national credit system, through which we had absolute national sovereignty over banking, monetary, and financial policy for the purpose of consciously and deliberately fostering human advancement. The primary mission of Hamilton's national bank was to increase the rate of development of the physical economy through new scientific breakthroughs and new internal improvements, and technologies to increase the productivity of labor.

Today, both the Federal Reserve and our "modern" banking and financial system operate solely on the basis of maximizing private monetary profit, with the day-to-day operations of this system driven by usurious and speculative monetary schemes. This is a system axiomatically the opposite of how Hamilton's national bank functioned.

As Hamilton stresses again and again in his reports, the *primary* function of the national bank—unlike the Federal Reserve, the Bank of England and all current central banks—was to *make loans for productive enterprise*. Under strict U.S. Treasury supervision, the national bank operated as a commercial bank, accepting deposits from the public and making loans to private citizens and businesses. The national bank established branches in nine cities, including in almost all of the manufacturing and commercial centers. From these branches, credit flowed into the productive physical economy. As deposits accumulated in the national bank, investments were made in new manufacturing, and farmers were given the ability to make improvements to their land.

Unlike today's Federal Reserve, Hamilton's national bank was a bulwark against financial speculation, and it did not act as a lender of last resort for unsound private banks or financiers. Hamilton stated that it would be the policy "to succor the wary and industrious; to discredit the rash and unthrifty; to discountenance both usurious lenders and usurious borrowers."

The axiomatic basis of Hamilton's approach, and what became known as the American System, is the understanding that the ultimate source of all wealth comes from mankind's creative discoveries. Money has no intrinsic value, but must be used as a tool to facilitate the creation of true value through human enterprise. As Hamilton wrote,

> The intrinsic wealth of a nation is to be measured, not by the abundance of the precious metals contained in it, but by the quantity of the productions of its labor and industry. ... The tendency of the national bank is to increase public and private credit. Industry is increased, commodities are multiplied, agriculture and manufactures flourish, and herein consist the true wealth and prosperity of the state.

The full intention of Hamilton's system is revealed in his 1791 *Report on the Subject of Manufactures*. What Hamilton presents in this work is an extended argument in favor of scientific, technological and industrial progress as the foundation of the sovereign nation state and the basis for the advancement of the people.

A careful reading of this report reveals that the primary intention of the national bank—together with Hamilton's other initiatives in tariffs, taxation, and internal improvements—is to foster rapid advances in upward human development. Everything is designed to serve the interests of the people, to create more opportunity, and to support the inventiveness and creativity of the citizenry. As Hamilton says in the report, "to cherish and stimulate the activity of the human mind, by multiplying the objects of enterprise, is not among the least considerable of the expedients by which the wealth of a nation may be promoted."

REPORT ON MANUFACTURES

COMMUNICATION TO THE
HOUSE OF REPRESENTATIVES
DECEMBER 5, 1791

FROM

ALEXANDER HAMILTON
SECRETARY OF THE TREASURY

ON THE
SUBJECT OF MANUFACTURES

Hamilton proceeds to define a series of measures to actively promote the manufacturing and technological development of the nation, including:

1. Protective Tariffs

2. The Prohibition of Rival Articles [restricting imports of goods that compete with domestically produced items]

3. Premiums and Pecuniary Bounties [using tariff revenue to sponsor new inventions and technologies]

4. The Encouragement of New Inventions and Discoveries

5. The Facilitating of the Transportation of Commodities

For Hamilton, the purpose of tariffs is primarily to protect and promote the development of *new* industries and *new* productive capabilities. As to transportation, Hamilton proposes an active role by the national government in developing the nation's transportation systems, including ports, canals and roads (often referred to as internal improvements, at the time). But, in his proposals for bounties, premiums, and the encouragement of new inventions and discoveries, Hamilton goes even further. He is defining new industries, new inventions, and new discoveries as the indispensable pathway for the economic betterment of the nation. This is an active, not passive, use of the institutions of government to support human advancement through creative and productive enterprise.

Hamilton also proposes the establishment of a national "development board," which shall be instituted to:

> Promote the introduction of useful discoveries, inventions and improvements by proportional rewards, judiciously held out and applied; to encourage by premiums, both honorable and lucrative, the exertions of individuals and of classes, in relation to the several objects they are charged with promoting; and to afford such other aids to those objects as may be generally designated by law, [and to encourage the] emigration of artists and manufacturers in particular branches of extraordinary importance.

This is a nation-building policy and a path to national prosperity. This American System approach has nothing to do with silly notions of socialism or communism, and is in explicit opposition to free-trade doctrines developed by the British Empire to justify their global imperial control and looting policies. It's about ensuring our nation has sovereign control over our credit system, and is able to use credit and other tools to protect and encourage human creative advancement as the only true source of wealth.

Returning to the American System

On June 19, 2024, President Donald Trump posted a short statement on Truth Social:

> If you want to study Tariffs, and how powerful they are, study the administration of President William McKinley. America had so much money they didn't know what to do with it!

Prior to the mid-20th century and for most of American history, high tariff rates were a cornerstone of American economic policy. Prior to the adoption of the Constitution, tariffs, or the lack thereof, were the leading source of economic contention, as well as a major cause of the new nation's fiscal crisis under the Articles of Confederation. Without a new Constitution, states were in a race to the bottom over lower and lower tariffs in hopes of monopolizing trade, which, as a result, would deprive the nation of critical resources to pay the army, to retire the debt, and to fund the post-war recovery. One of the first acts of Congress in 1789, under the new Constitution, was to apply to the new unified nation a uniform impost tax on imports.

Alexander Hamilton introduced a national policy of protective tariffs. Later, in the 19th century, a series of American System presidents—most notably John Quincy Adams, Abraham Lincoln and William McKinley—would expand on this approach. From 1789 to 1950, tariff rates

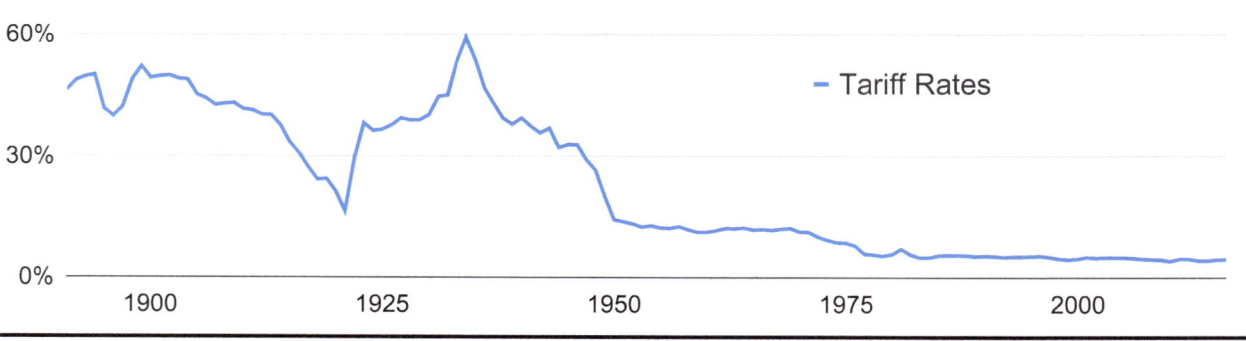

almost never dipped below 20 percent, and there were extended periods when tariffs of 40 to 50 percent were in effect.

For 40 years, from 1861 through 1901, tariff rates averaged over 45 percent. This was the "era of American protectionism," and its chief champion was Congressman and later President William McKinley. In recent decades, it has become fashionable to dismiss tariffs as woefully outmoded relics of a bygone era, but the reality is that they worked magnificently. Between 1861 and 1901, the United States created the greatest industrial revolution in human history, one which permeated every aspect of manufacturing, agriculture, energy and infrastructure. During those 40 years, income from the tariffs accounted for anywhere between 33 percent and 50 percent of all federal revenue (while the personal income tax was basically nonexistent).

Disastrous Modern Free Trade Era

President Franklin Roosevelt is often portrayed as anti-tariff, but this is simply not true. Yes, he opposed the 1930 Smoot-Hawley Tariff and, after 1934, he marginally reduced tariff rates. But, at the time of Roosevelt's death in 1945, U.S. tariff rates still averaged 38 percent, almost double what had existed under Woodrow Wilson in 1920.

It was under Harry Truman that everything began to change. In 1947, the United States became a founding member of the General Agreement on Trade and Tariffs (GATT). Between 1947 and 1950, in just three years, U.S. tariff rates were slashed from more than 35 percent down to 14 percent; then, they continued to ratchet down to less than 5 percent by 1975.

A historic U.S. trade surplus had started in 1870, driven by tariffs and rapid industrial advancement, and peaking around 1920. By 1970, we had a trade deficit, and, in 1971, that trade deficit contributed to major shocks to the global financial system, leading President Nixon to take the dollar off the gold reserve. This initiated the disastrous modern global free trade and financial deregulation era.

In January 1995, the United States became a founding member of the World Trade Organization, ushering in the last 30-year era of radical free trade, which led to the almost complete disappearance of large-scale manufacturing inside the United States. This was the new paradigm of deindustrialization and globalization. Elites imposed a policy in which our nation abandoned its heritage as a nation of producers, becoming a nation reliant on imports produced by cheap labor (exactly what our Founding Fathers feared). Without a regulated and protective U.S. trade and financial system, the central bank and national income tax regime became increasingly oppressive for the American people, with higher inflation, higher trade deficits, and lower wages.

President Trump has publicly expressed interest in the recent proposal to enact a 10 percent general tariff on all imports, and has suggested rates as high as 20 percent. Some have

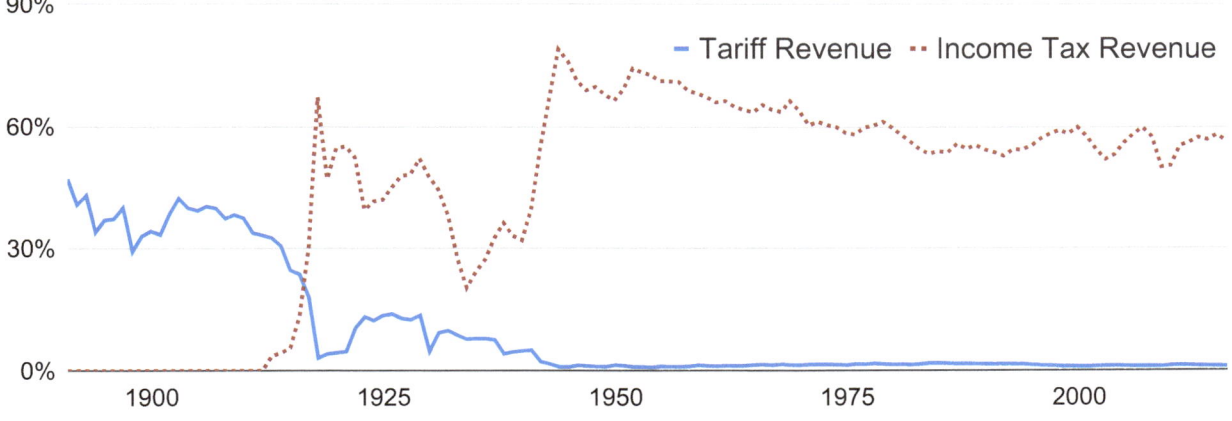

Tariffs vs Personal Income Tax as Percentage of Total Federal Revenue

denounced this, but, in reality, a 10 percent tariff would merely return us to the already very low tariff rate of 1960. Promethean Action endorses the 10 percent tariff, but also suggests that key areas of American industry and technology will require higher rates of protection.

It is also vitally important to recognize that tariffs alone will not solve our problems. Without public credit and national banking, no in-depth economic recovery is possible. Additionally, the roadblocks that have been erected within the United States to prohibit productive economic investment—many of them an outgrowth of radical environmentalism—must be fully removed.

Public Credit Today

Today, we suffer under a banking and financial system that is dominated by the obsession with usurious monetarist thinking and the pursuit of short-term monetary profits. Little, if any, thought is expended by our financial elites on the urgent necessity to build up a vibrant productive economy. Many of our current catastrophic financial practices can be traced back to the so-called financial deregulation of the 1990s, including, but not limited to, the repeal of the Glass-Steagall Act of 1933 and the passage of the insane Gramm–Leach–Bliley Act in 1999, which dismantled the very firewall that stood between speculative investment banking and commercial banks. The role of the Federal Reserve, particularly since the 2008-2009 financial crisis, has also greatly exacerbated the transformation of our banking and financial system into a giant shell of pure financial speculation. Alexander Hamilton must be howling from his grave, having to witness what fools have done to our Constitutional system of productive public credit.

We need to reimpose Glass-Steagall banking provisions and take all other necessary measures to build an iron wall separating useful productive investment from pure financial speculation. We need to rebuild our system of private banks throughout the nation, freeing them from the speculative financial merry-go-round and returning them to their traditional productive role.

We need to escape from the mental trap of funding critical projects out of the federal government's general fund and, then, complaining about "budget deficits." Instead, we should re-learn Hamilton's approach to public credit. It is possible that new credit facilities could be established, tailored to specific projects or areas of needed investment. For example, something like a Baseload Energy Bank could be established to finance energy projects at discounted rates, with bonds purchased by the American people. We need to start thinking in this way.

We need to return to the system of sovereign national banking. Look at how Abraham Lincoln utilized Greenbacks to industrialize and develop the nation during the Civil War, including funding half of the Transcontinental Railroad. Study how President Franklin Roosevelt used the Reconstruction Finance Corporation as a vehicle to use public credit to construct vitally needed and useful projects during the Great Depression.

But, above all, to ensure that any of these American System policies are successful, we have to understand the underlying principles. Under the American System, public credit can be thought of as borrowing from the future increases in productivity which are the unique products of human creativity and human enterprise. In the concluding section of this pamphlet, we unveil new insights into the little-understood secrets underlying mankind's unique capabilities. But first, let's see how we can revive and expand these policies today as the American System 2.0.

Join our campaign for The American System 2.0

A growing coalition of Americans is fighting for economic growth through a revival of the American System of Economics.

Prom.ac/AmSys2

American System Case Study: The Reconstruction Finance Corporation

The Reconstruction Finance Corporation (RFC) was a quasi-public corporation established in 1932 to deal with the crisis of the Great Depression. The RFC was owned by the federal government, which appointed the corporation's executive officers and board of directors, but was staffed by professionals recruited outside of the civil service system, and its borrowings and expenditures were independent (off-budget) of the federal government budget. Thus, RFC expenditures did not increase budget deficits. The RFC was empowered to make loans and finance projects without Congressional approval. The initial funding for the RFC came from the sale of $500 million worth of stocks and bonds to the United States Treasury. To obtain more capital, it sold $1.5 billion in bonds to the Treasury, which then sold them to the general public. Over the period from 1932 through 1941, the RFC loaned or otherwise disbursed about $9.5 billion. By the time the RFC was dissolved in 1957, it was "in the black" and had repaid all of its loans from the federal government, as well as other creditors. A full discussion of the myriad of projects and initiatives which the RFC undertook is beyond the scope of this pamphlet, but during the Depression years, the RFC built an unparalleled economic juggernaut, financing rural electrification, water management, dams, bridges, etc., much of which was accomplished through collaboration with state and local authorities. The RFC was a public credit institution and it worked. It built up the productive power of the economy and helped to create a skilled workforce, without costing the nation a penny.

Norris Dam construction, 1936. Tennessee Valley Authority historic collection (image cropped, CC BY 2.0).

Part 2 — Science of Negentropic Economic Growth

The American System 2.0

Today, we can ensure the United States becomes a manufacturing superpower and provides a better future for our population and our posterity with the American System 2.0. Hamilton identified the axiomatic basis for the American System when he said, "the intrinsic wealth of a nation is to be measured, not by the abundance of the precious metals contained in it, but by the quantity of the products of its labor and industry." The great American physical economist Lyndon LaRouche (1922-2019) provided, 200 years later, a new understanding of how we can increase the quantity of the products of our labor and industry through his development of a science of physical economics.

Lyndon LaRouche speaking in 1985.

This approach is fundamentally different from more traditional studies of supply and demand or market fluctuations. Those traditional studies have their place when examining the shorter term variations in the exchanges of goods and services, but they fail to address the fundamental nature of long-term economic growth. We're talking about the big changes that determine the fate of entire generations, the deeper changes that can ensure each new generation is better off than their parents' generation, the type of progress that made America great and can make America great again.

The central basis for understanding economics as a physical science is to define, understand, and measure the factors which determine changes in the so-called carrying capacity of a society.[1] For example, it would be impossible for the current world population of 8 billion people to be supported in an economy based on pre-industrial revolution technologies; and it would have been impossible for the world population of one billion people in 1800 to be supported in an economy based on pre-agricultural revolution technologies. Those are examples of changes on the very largest scales of human development, but the same fundamental issues are at play in the year-to-year policy decisions of individual nations. For reasons explained shortly below, we'll identify this type of progress specifically as *negentropic economic growth* (to distinguish these changes from more traditional measures of economic growth, such as GDP, etc.).

As the original American System proponents understood, these changes come from the unique human capability for scientific discovery and cultural advance. When expressed through technology, these changes

1. The more technical term developed for this by Mr. LaRouche is *potential relative population density*.

increase the ability of the labor force to produce what's needed to support society—increasing what Hamilton called the *productive power of labor*. Further, the so-called natural resources that are the basis for the operations of an entire economy are not fixed. What is and is not available for use as a natural resource is determined by the level of science, technology, and culture of a society.

In the late-1970s, Mr. LaRouche developed a framework to assess if an economy is growing (negentropic) or collapsing (entropic) in physical terms.[2] We start by dividing the entire population into two groups: first, *productive labor households*, which include the population living in households whose primary wage-earner is employed in the production of useful, tangible output in agriculture, manufacturing, construction, mining, energy production, and freight transport; second, the households supporting the rest of the population (those households whose primary wage-earner is not engaged in production of the first type) or *overhead households*.[3] We're identifying the physical goods that society requires to survive and isolating the section of the labor force responsible for their production.

---

2. Here we're largely following: LaRouche, Lyndon H. Jr., *Why Credit Can Be Greatly Expanded Without Adding to Inflation*, New York, National Democratic Policy Committee, 1980; and, from 1984, LaRouche, Lyndon H. Jr., *So, You Wish to Learn All About Economics?*, New York, New Benjamin Franklin House, second edition, 1995.
3. Within overhead, we could also further distinguish between categories of overhead that are necessary and indispensable vs those that are wasteful.

The traditional economic metric of GDP includes the "value" of wasteful activities (including legalized drug sales, prostitution, and gambling, to cite some extreme examples) which can be meaningless, if not outright destructive, to the ability of an economy to sustain itself in physical terms. By the GDP approach, we're measuring the volume of total economic activity, regardless of whether the activity contributes to what's needed to sustain society physically. By Mr. LaRouche's physical economic approach, we're focusing on the section of the labor force directly involved in producing what's needed to keep society running in physical terms, *allowing us to isolate and examine what causes changes in their ability to produce those goods.*

Because these necessary physical goods are both the input provided to the productive labor force and the output of their productive activities, *this creates the basis to measure an economy as if it were a thermodynamic system*. We separate the total physical output of the productive labor force into different categories, based on how those tangible goods are to be used. We're first interested in the ability of the productive labor force to produce the so-called *energy of the system*—*the physical goods required to keep society running at its present technological level*—vs the production of additional *free energy*—*the physical goods available to invest in new areas and new upgrades (the net operating profit for the economy as a whole).*

This view of the economy, as if it were a closed thermodynamic process, allows us to isolate and understand what causes changes in the ability of the productive labor force to produce the

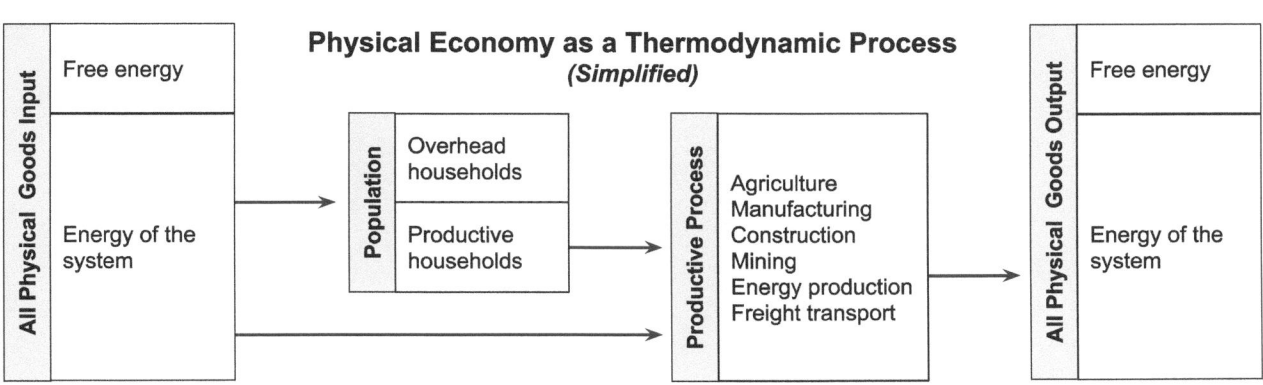

tangible goods that keep the economy going in physical terms. Without first defining this type of framework, any notion of economic value is arbitrary, as we need to measure the actions of productive labor relative to the requirements to sustain society. Only with this type of approach can we begin to define and understand economic growth in terms of a physical science.

To distinguish our physical economic metrics from the arbitrary metrics often used, we define ***negentropic economic growth*** as the ability for the productive labor force to provide the required energy of the system, plus a higher level of free energy than was produced in the previous cycle.[4] Over successive cycles, this will be expressed as an increasing energy of the system as the economy realizes the fruits of negentropic growth. In the remainder of this section, we'll outline the key areas where such negentropic growth can be generated, outlining the path for a bright and prosperous future for our nation for generations to come.

First, we address manufacturing from an emphasis on technological progress and the closely related factors of *energy flux-density* and *capital intensity*. Through the utilization of new technologies operating at higher energy flux-densities and increasing the concentration of useful tools and machinery (capital goods) employed by the labor force, we can ensure America becomes a manufacturing superpower again. This is the secret to ensuring that a tariff policy works.

Second, we examine how economic infrastructure defines the physical economic spacetime in which production occurs. Lowering the cost while increasing the availability and quality of energy, water, and transportation for productive enterprises ensures those productive enterprises can operate at overall higher levels of productivity. Public credit becomes a key tool to enable these types of long-term investments.

Everything President Trump has presented in his economic program is in the right direction. However, it is just the very beginning of an economic revival for our nation and a cultural renaissance celebrating the true nature of mankind. Mr. LaRouche's work defining a science of physical economics provides the basis to advance the original American System into what we call the American System 2.0, ensuring we can revive a commitment to long-term, negentropic progress over the next generation and beyond.

---

4. In reality, the economy obviously isn't a closed system, and we also have to account for changes (both negative and positive) in the natural resources available at any given technological level. This is taken up in detail below.

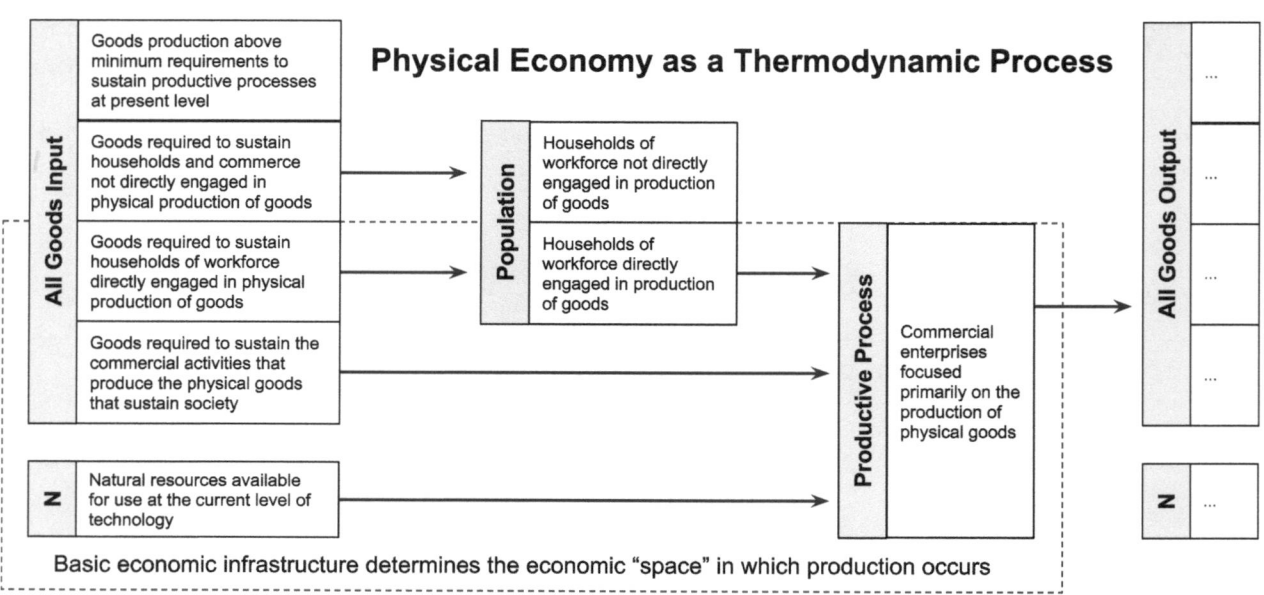

How to Become a Manufacturing Superpower: Technology and the Productive Powers of Labor

In many respects, America is fast approaching the condition of a Third World, developing nation. We have lost hundreds of thousands of factories. Go into a Wal-Mart, a Home Depot, or shop on Amazon and you will find almost everything is imported, and what is left of our manufacturing sector, like the automobile and aerospace industries, likewise is dependent on imports. Look at the machines being employed; look at the individual parts used in the final product; look at the bolts, the machine tools, the electronic components. Almost all are made overseas. This is also true of the defense sector, where the question of foreign supply chains becomes a matter of national security. We are vulnerable as a nation.

As President Trump and others realize, we can and must use tariffs and other American System measures to bring manufacturing production back to America. But, the secret to making this work is to rapidly increase the productive powers of our labor force, ensuring domestically produced goods are of the highest quality and manufactured at the highest levels of productivity. This means new technologies, higher capital intensity, and higher levels of energy flux-density—concepts few understand today.

To see what true productivity increase looks like, look at the long-term changes in agriculture. We went from requiring 95 percent of our labor force to be engaged in agriculture at the time of the American Revolution, to only 2 percent today. How was such a revolutionary transformation possible? At the founding of our nation, farmers had relatively simple tools, powered only by human and animal physical power, leading to a relatively low level of productivity per farmer. At these productivity levels, the majority of the population had to be engaged in agriculture simply to feed the nation.

Then, in the 18th century, steam engines and heat-powered machinery were introduced, powering the Industrial Revolution. Industrial mass-production put more tools into the hands of the farmer (capital intensity), including tools that embodied higher technologies. This included the use of heat-powered machinery in tractors and farm equipment directly used by the farmer, which increased the quantity and concentration of energy applied to the agricultural productive process (energy flux-density). Further, water projects ensured stable freshwater supplies, while the expansion of rail networks enabled the cheap transportation of capital

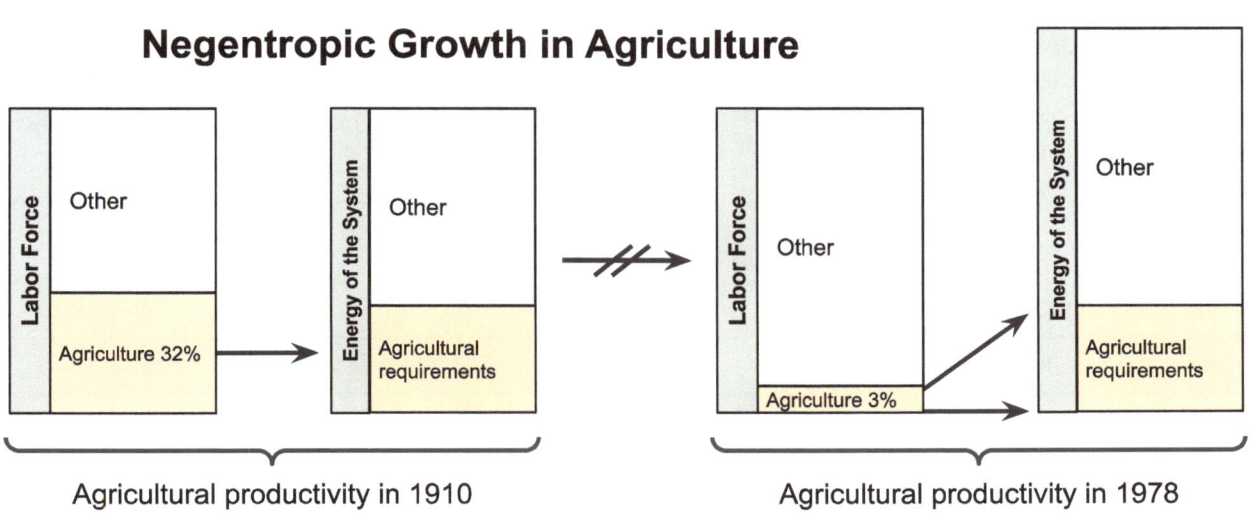

Promethean Action

goods to the farmers and the cheap transportation of their products to various markets (infrastructure). Together with improvements in land management and fertilizers, the average farmer's productive power of labor increased by leaps and bounds.

After a century as a nation, the percentage of the labor force that needed to be engaged in agriculture just to feed the population dropped from 95 percent to 50 percent. After World War II, it was down to 10 percent, and today it's at 2 percent. Stated another way, in 1910, each farmworker produced enough food to support 9 people. By 1978, each individual farmworker could sustain 65 people with the fruits of their labor. This is an excellent example of negentropic growth: *increasing productive powers of labor enabled a steady decline in the percentage of the labor force required to produce the agricultural components of the energy of the system.*

Negentropic growth isn't created by employing large numbers of people cheaply; it's created by increasing the productive powers of labor of an educated and skilled workforce. Let's look at how we utilize these principles to accelerate our return to being a manufacturing superpower.

Natural Resources, Raw Materials, and Energy Flux-Density

According to a 2024 *Mineral Commodity Summaries Report* by the United States Geological Survey, the United States is now reliant on imports for more than one-half of the country's consumption of 49 minerals, and 100 percent import-dependent for 15 of them. China continues to be the top supplier of the minerals that the U.S. needs, and it dominates the global production and export of minerals, such as rare earth elements, graphite, and lithium, which are vital for the energy, manufacturing, technology, transportation, infrastructure, and defense.

We obviously can't cover every raw material here, so let's focus on one of the most important raw materials for a modern economy: iron ore for steel production.[1] Vital components of the U.S. economy—from heavy machinery manufacturing, shipbuilding, heavy construction, power plant construction, railway construction, etc.—are dependent on steel production, and expanding our economy will require a massive increase. To build 200 one-gigawatt nuclear power plants will require 6 to 7 million metric tons of steel. To build a modern freight and passenger rail system requires 175 tons of steel per mile. And the continental water project, the North American Water and Power Alliance (NAWAPA), would require an estimated 300 million tons of steel to construct. The question of steel production is a matter of both national security and the overall ability of the United States to successfully progress into the future.

Before the failed policies of the past two generations, the U.S. was a world leader in steel production. How did we get there? Our history of iron and steel production provides an excellent demonstration of physical economic principles required for reviving the production of steel and other raw materials at the highest levels of productivity and efficiency ever seen.

In 1830, the average U.S. iron and steel worker produced 10 tons per year. By 1900, productivity leaped to 70 tons per worker per year. By 1970, it reached 180 tons per worker per year. These

---

1. Steel production and consumption has been recognized as a general proxy for economic growth. As the primary element in steel, iron is, by far, the most produced element of the periodic table by weight.

	Productivity of Workers (tons output / worker / year)	Productivity of Energy (tons output / billion BTUs)	Energy Flux-Density (million BTUs / m² / hour)
Charcoal era (1830)	10	4	3
Carnegie era (1900)	70	45	10
Space era (1970)	170	80	27
The future	??	~250	~340

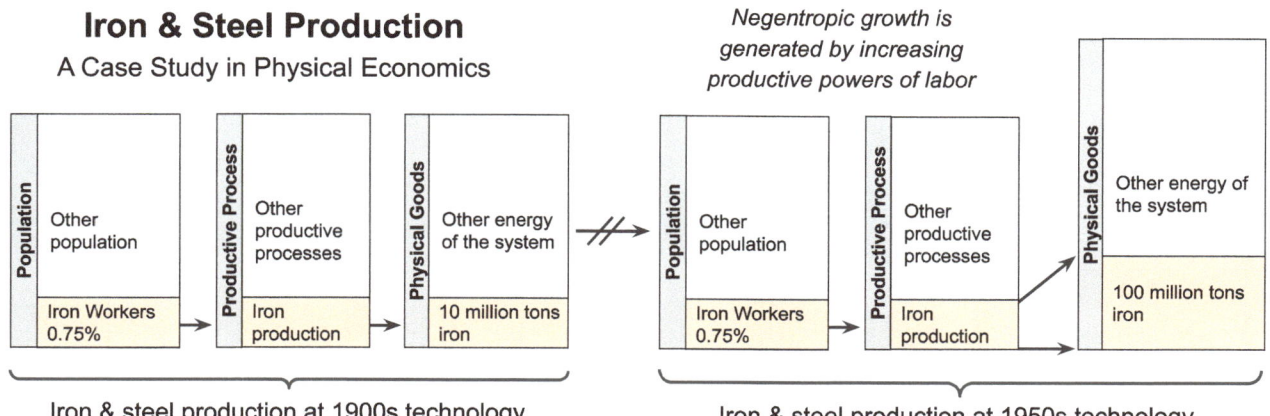

Iron & Steel Production
A Case Study in Physical Economics

Negentropic growth is generated by increasing productive powers of labor

Iron & steel production at 1900s technology

Iron & steel production at 1950s technology

massive productivity upshifts were associated with an array of unique technological advancements (shifting to higher quality coal, adding coke, introducing oxygen blast furnaces, computer controlled systems, etc). But the invariant to every technological upshift was the increasing energy flux-density of the mode of production (measuring the concentration and intensity of energy used in the productive process).

With each new technology, not only did the total energy applied increase, but, more importantly, the concentration of the energy throughput (the energy flux-density) increased—tripling between 1830 and 1900, and tripling again from 1900 to 1970. *Energy flux-density is a key metric for technological advance and increasing productive powers of labor.*

This type of progress is indispensable for negentropic growth, as the total annual steel production was able to leap by orders of magnitude, from one million tons in 1880, to 10 million tons in 1900, to 100 million tons in 1950, *while the percentage of the labor force employed in steel production was nearly constant, at about 0.75%, across the entire time.* This is negentropic growth: an expanding energy of the system (to support an advancing economy) is sustained by a fixed percentage of the labor force. This would have never happened without the use of strong tariffs during this period.

Already in the 1980s, plasma separation technologies were being developed that operated at double (or more) the energy flux-density, holding the possibility of massive gains in output per worker. Today, new methods of steel production, solely by electricity (through electrolysis), could be another revolutionary game changer. Future technologies for raw materials processing at higher energy flux-densities won't be limited to steel production, but can ensure efficient and economical domestic production of a wide variety of key minerals and raw materials. A massive increase in energy supply at substantially lower costs is key, and we will return to that point in our discussion of infrastructure, below.

Creating New Natural Resources

There is another dimension to these advances that requires special emphasis: *increases in the so-called natural resources available.* In reality, the term "natural resources" is a terrible misnomer, as the decisive factor that determines if something is or is not a useful resource is the level of science and technology developed and applied throughout your society. As we'll focus on in the concluding section of this pamphlet, such revolutions are the basis for a cultural optimism celebrating a newfound appreciation for the notion of mankind as a unique creative force in the universe.

With advanced (specifically high energy flux-density) modes of production, deposits currently considered to be low quality or useless can become economical and profitable. We've seen this quite clearly in the energy sector with fracking (hydraulic fracturing) and other advanced oil and gas extraction technologies, which have opened up massive deposits that

New Science & Technology Changes the Resources Available to Mankind

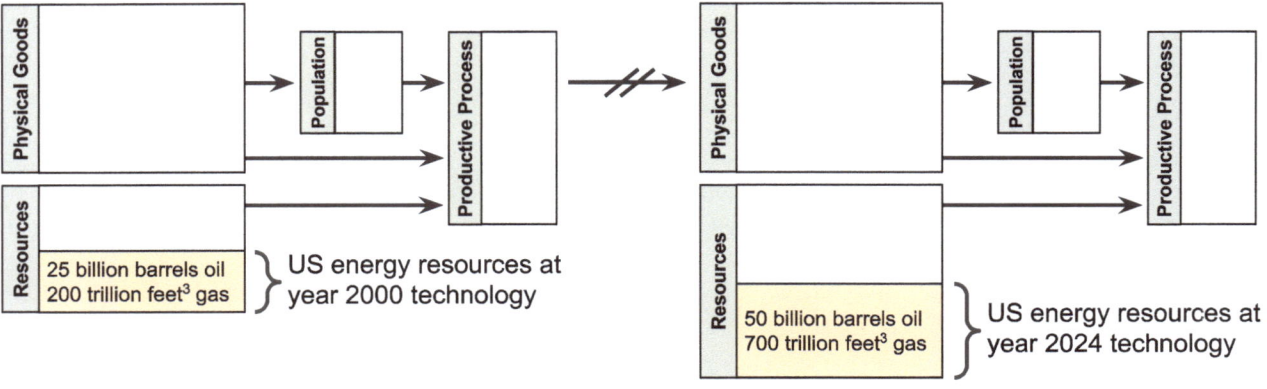

were considered practically worthless before. In the U.S., from 2000 to today, proved reserves of oil increased from 25 billion barrels to nearly 50 billion barrels, and proved reserves of natural gas have increased from 200 trillion cubic feet to 700 trillion cubic feet.

The same can become true for a wide variety of minerals and raw materials. For example, large regions of Oregon and Washington in the Pacific Northwest contain massive deposits of aluminum ores (laterite) with concentrations generally one fifth to one half that of currently used aluminum ores (bauxite). With present technologies, these massive deposits are worthless, but, with higher energy flux-density technologies, these will become accessible and profitable deposits. The same is true for iron ores for steel production. Current ores are about 25 percent iron, while average soil is about 5 percent iron. With appropriate technological advancements, that soil becomes a resource for iron ore. Those aren't unique or special examples. All natural resources are defined by the level of science and technology effectively employed in a physical economy, meaning there are no inherent limits to natural resources, only limits imposed by a given level of technology. When we say a properly functioning public credit system borrows against future increases in wealth and productivity, this is an excellent example.

Many aspects of securing U.S. domestic raw material production are of immediate priority for a second Trump administration: protecting and expanding U.S. steel production, expanding America's mining and mineral capabilities, and cutting the absurd bureaucratic and radical environmental red tape that stands in the way.[2] But, generating long-term progress and prosperity also requires initiatives that drive future technological advance, with a heavy emphasis on increasing energy flux-density for processing mineral natural resources into the raw materials that feed the economy. Only this can ensure both secure domestic supplies and negentropic growth to provide new levels of prosperity.

Manufacturing, Machine Tools, and Technology

For the 50 year period from 1920 to 1970, U.S. manufacturing consistently accounted for 20 percent to 30 percent of GDP. Today, it's only 10 percent. For decades, ivory tower academic economists teamed up with the Washington, DC elite to champion our transition to a post-industrial, so-called services economy, placing us in an incredibly vulnerable situation where we simply don't produce what we need to survive. The disruption and collapse of various vital supply chains during the 2020 COVID-19 outbreak was a harsh wakeup call. Many are familiar with our reliance on foreign supplies

---

2. The National Mining Association states that it now can take 7 to 10 years to secure federal approvals for mines in the United States, while it takes just two to three years in countries like Australia and Canada.

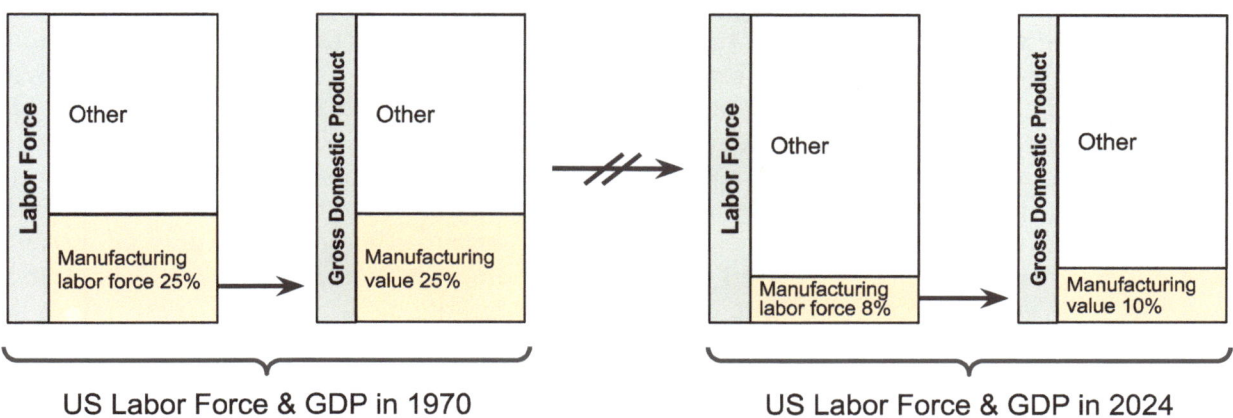

Domestic Manufacturing Collapse since 1970

for semiconductors, rare earth elements, and pharmaceutical drugs, but those are just a few of many examples.

To reverse this disastrous trend, we can't simply reshore existing manufacturing factories and technologies. We must look to the frontier technologies that will ensure the highest possible leaps in productivity. The past decades' focus on cheap-labor manufacturing was a costly mistake, and our future depends on the development of a new creative and innovative manufacturing sector, developing and employing new technologies. *This is the secret of ensuring that a tariff policy works, protecting the development of new technologies that increase the productive powers of labor.*

There is already a lot of interest in the frontier technologies of advanced robotics (including humanoid robots), artificial intelligence, and quantum computers. However, greater emphasis needs to be placed on how these technologies can enhance the ability of the productive labor force to increase the ratio of free energy production in the economy. If these technologies are primarily employed in the service sector or a services-dominated economy, without a shift of the overall economy back towards physical production of useful goods, then what they contribute will be largely meaningless, and our economy will continue to decline. The context for technology must always be the physical economy, as illustrated by LaRouche's thermodynamic approach.

Machines That Make Machines

Many Americans have no comprehension of the life-or-death importance of machine tools to the continued development of a productive economy. Machine tools are the machines that produce the machines that produce the goods. For the 35 years following World War II, the United States led the world in machine tool design and production. Today, we're fourth or fifth, behind China, Japan, and Germany. Today, imported machine tools make up 67 percent of U.S. consumption. In some critical sectors, this rises to 100 percent.

Any attempt to make America once again a manufacturing superpower will require a dramatic upgrading and expansion of the nation's machine tool capabilities, as well as the recruitment of young, dedicated, and skilled trainees to operate them. Machine tools are not only necessary for a productive economy, they play a unique role in transmitting negentropic growth when they're used to produce new generations of machines or machines which operate at higher levels of technology.

To a significant degree, any program of negentropic growth hinges on an advanced machine tool capacity. The issue is not merely a domestic ability to create the machines we need to manufacture goods (although that is part of it), the critical factor is the ability to rapidly and efficiently create new generations of productive machinery which incorporate the new technologies that increase the productive powers of the labor force. Making America, once again, the leading manufacturing and technological superpower in the world will necessitate trillions of dollars of investment in a broad range of very challenging projects: nuclear power plants, water desalination, high-speed rail systems, the space program, and countless other medium- and small-scale projects. This requires breakthroughs in technology, new machines, new parts, and new components, many based on designs that have yet to be created. None of this can be done without an advanced machine tool sector and a highly skilled workforce, fostered by American System measures, such as tariffs.

The machine tool sector represents a unique interface between the ultimate increase in the productive powers of labor, which represent negentropic growth (in effects), and the uniquely human scientific and technological discoveries, which are the ultimate source of wealth (the cause). In the machine tool sector, engineers implement scientific discoveries in new machine designs, connecting the creativity of an individual mind to the physical economic capabilities of an entire society. This is an illustration of the absolute distinction of mankind from the animals (despite what corrupt academics and radical environmentalists may argue) and the universal importance of human progress.

The Urgent Requirement to Rebuild a Skilled Workforce

Extensive efforts are needed to retrain and rebuild a highly productive, technologically advanced labor force. Under 50 years of a policy of deindustrialization, our productive manufacturing economy has been replaced by a weak and vulnerable service economy. More recently, the new gig economy has encompassed somewhere between 10 percent to 36 percent of the nation's total workforce, complete with side hustles, temporary jobs, and a plethora of consultants. The vast majority of these workers lack healthcare benefits and savings, and they are unable to form and support new families. More than two-thirds of our workforce are now employed in the services economy, meaning our ratio of overhead households to productive households is way out of whack: we no longer have the productive labor force needed to maintain our energy of the system requirements. Part of what is required is simply training the younger workforce. This can include a massive expansion and improvement of several approaches already in existence, including STEM education (science, technology, engineering, and mathematics), the educational programs associated with the Army Corps of Engineers, and programs of a number of other institutions. This can involve partnerships between the private sector, state and local government, the U.S. military, and federal agencies, such as the Department of Energy. The Corps of Engineers, which employs 37,000 civilians and soldiers, is situated to play a vital role in making America great again. Its public engineering program is premier in the world, and its educational programs provide training in engineering and construction crucial to the infrastructure projects our nation requires. An expansion of these efforts would produce great benefits in the recruitment and training of a new skilled workforce. Additionally, there is the U.S. military itself. There are currently more than 1,300,000 active duty servicemen and women, and another 800,000 in reserve forces. The various military branches already function, to one extent or another, as advanced schools in multiple areas of machine technology, engineering, and science. In addition to combat training and other military functions, young recruits are also exposed to advanced military technology (from aircraft, to drones, to satellite surveillance), requiring university-level training and skills. Military service is now dominated by three fields: mechanical and repair; engineering, science, and technical; and transportation and material handling. Thus, we can take advantage of this great potential, integrating it into the rebuilding of a productive workforce, as we act to shift our culture back to being a nation of producers.

Infrastructure as National Development
Energy, Power, Water, and Transportation

Infrastructure needs a special treatment and emphasis for three reasons. First, our infrastructure systems have been gravely neglected for decades, with the American Society of Civil Engineers grading our overall infrastructure a C- and reporting that $4.6 trillion in investments are required to get that grade to a B. Second, inflationary boondoggles like the Biden-Harris "Inflation Reduction Act" (just a front for the "Green New Deal") have been pushed on the American people under the name of "infrastructure," but these fake infrastructure programs have been disastrous for the economy. Third, and most importantly, infrastructure plays a unique role in defining the potential for productivity and the development of our national territory. Large-scale infrastructure systems transform entire territories, making uninhabitable regions inhabitable, and allowing unproductive regions to become productive.

Infrastructure systems are not products or goods in an economy, they define the potential for what can happen in an economy and where. Infrastructure determines the physical economic spacetime of an economy. As LaRouche wrote on the subject in 2010, "Man as a creator in the likeness of the great Creator, is expressed by humanity's creation of the 'artificial environments' we sometimes call 'infrastructure,' on which both the progress, and even the merely continued existence of civilized society depends."[1] The transformation of barren desert landscapes into highly productive regions where plant and animal life flourish alongside mankind is emblematic of the unique capabilities that define mankind as a special creative force in the universe (as the concluding section will show).

Here we'll focus on the importance of new large-scale projects for hig-speed rail, expanded fresh water supplies, and abundant cheap energy as an integrated perspective. Obviously, extensive work is also needed to repair existing roads, bridges, locks, dams, transmission lines, etc.; however, repairs to existing systems need to be situated within the context of a growth program to build the new infrastructure systems that support true negentropic growth. Again, an American System public credit approach is key, as these are 10 to 25 year investments to increase the overall productivity of our nation.

> "Man as a creator in the likeness of the great Creator, is expressed by humanity's creation of the 'artificial environments' we sometimes call 'infrastructure,' on which both the progress, and even the merely continued existence of civilized society depends."
>
> - Lyndon H. LaRouche Jr.

---

1. LaRouche, Lyndon H. Jr., "The Secret Economy," *Executive Intelligence Review*, Vol. 37, Number 21, May 28, 2010.

2021 Report Card for America's Infrastructure

American Society of Civil Engineers.

Transportation and High-speed Rail

The development of a nation is closely tied to its transportation systems, which act as the arteries and veins of an economy. Throughout the history of our nation, transportation megaprojects defined the development of our national territory: from the 1825 completion of the Erie Canal, connecting the Northeast to the Great Lakes and the Mississippi River; to the 1869 opening of the Transcontinental Railroad, connecting the eastern and western halves of the country; to President Eisenhower's Interstate Highway System, efficiently connecting every contiguous state in the nation. These projects defined our nation.

Today, we're in need of a national high-speed rail system for fast and efficient transport of freight and people throughout our territory. Modern high-speed rail technologies, including magnetic levitation trains, can operate at 300 miles per hour, ensuring goods and people can move throughout the economy quickly and efficiently. A comprehensive national high- speed rail network would provide a new level of economic integration between major cities and rural regions, where freight rates and schedules for smaller communities could match those of major markets.

Various existing proposals for high-speed rail networks should be reviewed, from initial regional networks to a full-scale national grid. Forget about slow and expensive initiatives like the California High-speed Rail project. The primary emphasis is to rapidly facilitate the transformation of the United States into a manufacturing superpower, with low costs and high speeds for the transport of raw materials, intermediate goods, and final goods throughout the entire economy.

Beyond improving the connectivity of existing regions of the economy, this will create new regions of economic activity with new towns and cities, especially when paired with expanded energy at lower costs and new freshwater supplies for the West. LaRouche emphasized the importance of creating "development corridors," where integrated corridors of high-speed transportation, abundant energy and power, fresh water, and high-speed communication systems create the potential for new towns and cities to emerge, and new productive enterprises to develop and flourish. This should include hundreds of thousands of new family farms throughout the entire country, ensuring the availability of locally-grown, high-quality food, production freed from the control of globalist food cartels.

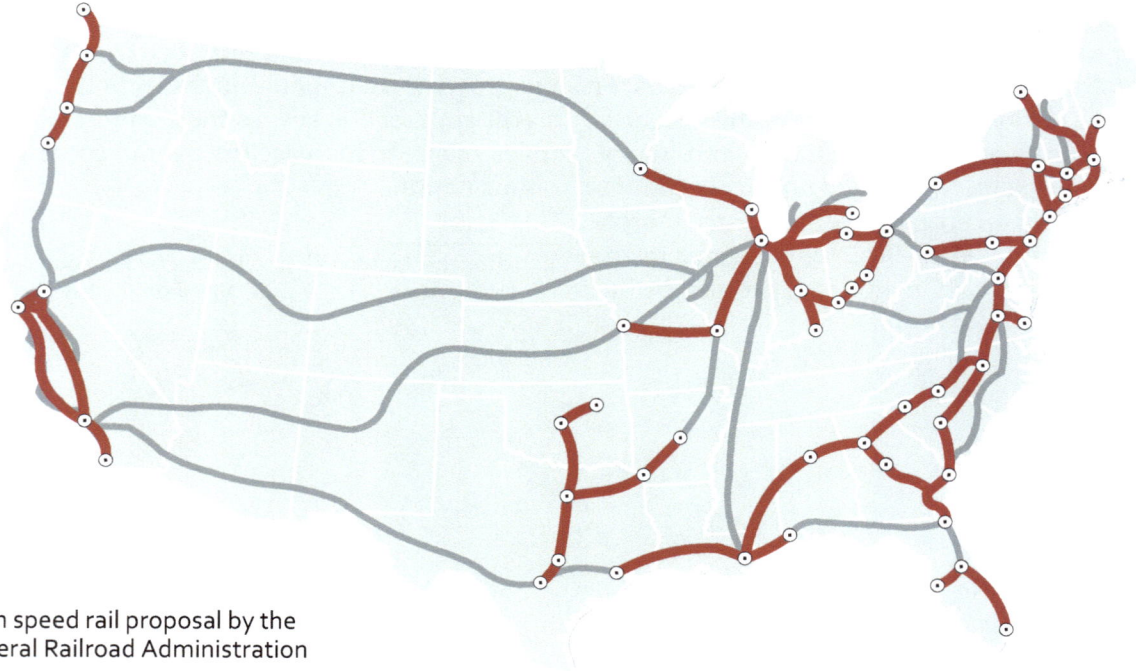

High speed rail proposal by the Federal Railroad Administration

Vast New Freshwater Supplies

The availability of fresh water has become a limiting factor for a major part of our nation. Over the past 25 years, an average of 43 percent of the United States was, at least, considered abnormally dry, and 26 percent was in some level of drought. Beyond drought for a quarter of our national territory, large regions of the country are dependent on underground aquifers that are being depleted. For example, between California's Central Valley, the Colorado River basin, and the Ogallala Aquifer (covering much of the Great Plains), groundwater stores are being withdrawn at rates faster than they're being replenished.

The rate of groundwater depletion throughout the Great Plains and the West is nearly comparable to having a second Colorado River flowing out of the ground—meaning this region is already in need of a second Colorado River just to break even in terms of water use (not accounting for growth). For decades, the West has faced recurring water emergencies, and serious measures to deal with the crisis can't wait any longer. Policies of conservation, recycling, and increasing efficiency can't address the core issue; we need to develop vast new supplies of fresh water for 25 percent to 40 percent of our nation's territory. The good news is that the necessary actions to resolve this crisis exist and are already known. There are two obvious ways to do this: coastal desalination projects and large-scale water transfer projects. Let's start with the grand vision for a continental-scale river management system designed in the 1960s and known as the North American Water and Power Alliance (NAWAPA).

The basic design of NAWAPA centers around balancing the irregularity of freshwater flows in the western half of our continent, with the Northwest (from Oregon to Alaska) having over 10 times the freshwater river runoff into the oceans as the Southwest (from California to Sinaloa in Mexico). NAWAPA was designed to mitigate this great western freshwater discrepancy by redirecting about 10 percent of total northwestern runoff (about 20 percent of a selection of rivers) throughout the Southwest United States and Northern Mexico. Canada would benefit with opportunities for economic development of untouched resources and abundant cheap hydroelectric power.[2]

The original NAWAPA design would bring the equivalent of 7 or 8 additional Colorado Rivers throughout the Southwest, ensuring that existing rivers in the region can be revitalized, groundwater stores could be replenished, and new territories can be developed.

---

2. See *NAWAPA XXI*, 2012 report by LaRouchePAC; and Deniston, Benjamin, "Solve the World Water Crisis," *Executive Intelligence Review*, Vol. 42, No. 5, January 30, 2015.

North American Water & Power Alliance (NAWAPA)

The largest challenges NAWAPA faces are the need for an agreement with Canada and the intense environmentalist opposition. At this point in time, the original 1960s NAWAPA design should be taken as a reference point, and the possible variations should be investigated, to either expand the overall project or streamline it to focus solely on United States territories (perhaps using piping through Canadian territories). Radical environmentalist regulations blocking or impeding large-scale water projects simply need to be eliminated. Whatever form it would take, a project to balance northwestern water abundance with southwestern water deficits isn't stealing from a finite supply of water, it's merely augmenting and improving the water cycle. It's taking fresh water that is already running off into the ocean, and redirecting a portion of it throughout the Southwest, where it can generate useful biological and economic activity before returning to the ocean to begin the cycle again. This could potentially increase the biospheric productivity of the *entire continent* by up to 10 percent.[3]

> The rate of groundwater depletion throughout the Great Plains and the West is nearly comparable to having a second Colorado River flowing out of the ground—meaning this region is already in need of a second Colorado River just to break even in terms of water use (not accounting for growth).

The second initiative to address the western water crisis is large-scale desalination to produce fresh water from ocean water. This is already being done elsewhere in the world, with the largest desalination plants being in Saudi Arabia and Israel. In California, the greater San Francisco Bay Area and the greater Los Angeles area account for two thirds of total urban water use in the state. To provide the entirety of these coastal urban water needs from ocean water would require less than two dozen desalination plants the size of Israel's largest plant, the Sorek (for comparison, California has more than 1,500 electric power plants). Being close to California's allocation of the Colorado River, this alone would be a significant step to reducing the demand on inland water supplies from the Colorado, San Joaquin, Sacramento, and other rivers.

That's just an initial example of what can be done. Desalination plants could be built with systems to pump the water further inland providing the freshwater requirements for non-coastal states. Again using Israel's Sorek desalination plant as a reference, 16 plants would match Arizona's allocation of the Colorado River, 10 would match Utah's

El Prat reverse osmosis desalination plant near Barcelona, Catalonia. Image credit: James Grellier (CC BY-SA 3.0).

---

3. This is assuming the new water is used at the same biospheric productivity level as the existing water supplies in the Southwest. See Deniston, Benjamin, "Solve the World Water Crisis," *Executive Intelligence Review*, Volume 42, Number 5, January 30, 2015.

allocation, and two would match Nevada's allocation. It must also be understood that all current arguments that begin with the phrase "desalination is too expensive" are fraudulent. The economics of scale and mass production of these facilities (if combined with the removal of environmental sabotage and lawsuits) will bring the costs down. But, most important is to recognize the nature of negentropic economic growth. This is another case of the revolutionary transformation of what we consider to be economically viable resources. With energy cost being a major factor for desalination, an expanded energy grid with lower power costs means the world's oceans become a natural resource for producing our freshwater needs for the foreseeable future.

Between large-scale water transfer with NAWAPA (or something similar) and large-scale desalination of ocean water, we can do much more than meet existing freshwater needs throughout the West. We can create the basis for additional growth and development. Currently, the Colorado River alone supports 40 million people, 16 million jobs, 5.7 million acres of farmland, and $1.4 trillion of annual economic activity. Imagine what more we can create with two to eight additional Colorado River's worth of fresh water. This is another excellent example where public credit would come into play, funding 10 to 25-year projects that would unleash the restricted economic productivity of 25 percent to 40 percent of our national territory.

Energy and Power

President Trump's call for "hundreds and hundreds and hundreds of big, beautiful power plants" is exactly on the right track. We must massively increase the availability of energy throughout the economy, while significantly lowering the costs. This will have profound impacts throughout every aspect of the economy.

Over the last several decades, U.S. baseline power-production has been decimated. A combination of deregulation, financialization, and "green" policies have created a situation where Third-World-style electricity brownouts and blackouts have become routine in many regions and where there is no energy capacity to actually grow the productive economy. Capital investment in natural gas and nuclear energy has dwindled, while "green" wind and solar projects, heavily backed by government subsidies and tax breaks, have given us the skyrocketing costs of the Harris/Biden "Green New Deal." As a result, the lights are going out and electricity prices keep rising.

Today, the per capita energy consumption for industry is less than it was in 1950.

The reconstruction of the United States as a "manufacturing superpower" will require enormous increased energy consumption by our industrial and manufacturing sectors, and frontier technologies, like artificial intelligence, require massive amounts of electricity. We should be planning to at least double electricity generation and increase our total energy generation by at least 50 percent.

One convenient way to look at the energy needs of our nation is to examine the energy flux-density of the economy as a whole. We do this by summing the total energy consumption (not only electricity) throughout all aspects of the economy (residential, commercial, industrial, and transportation) and divide that total by the number of people in the country to get a

Image credit: Hansueli Krapf (CC BY-SA 3.0).

measure of total energy consumption per person. This perspective gives us an ability to understand the contributions of different energy sources to the long-term growth of the economy.

The post-war economic boom through the early 1970s is expressed as a roughly 50 percent increase in economic energy flux-density. However, in the early 1970s, we had the beginning takeover of radical environmentalism and post-industrial policies (leading into globalization), and U.S. energy flux-density flatlined. Following the 2009 crisis, the downward trend accelerated (while President Trump's 2016 policies began to reverse this, the Biden administration put us right back on track toward disaster).

This stagnation and collapse in energy consumption has primarily been due to abandoning manufacturing. From 1950 to 1971, across all sectors (commercial, residential, transportation, and industry) there was a significant increase in energy consumption per person. Since the shift of the United States into a post-industrial services economy, per person energy consumption for industry collapsed, while the other three sectors all grew. From 1950 to 1971, energy for industry averaged nearly half of total energy consumption; today, it's less than a third. *Today, the per person energy consumption for industry is less than it was in 1950.*

This gives us a clear perspective on the massive energy requirements to return the United States to its status as a manufacturing superpower. Over the next 25 years, we should plan to increase the energy flux-density of the United States economy by 50 percent (mirroring the growth during the post-World War II economic boom). This will require:

- Eliminating the "Green New Deal" nonsense and related radical environmentalist policies, including the burdensome red tape and regulations hampering energy expansion.

- An immediate expansion of the use of oil and gas and clean coal (as some of the cheapest and most rapidly-deployable sources of electricity and heat energy for industry and transportation).

- Rapid efforts to standardize and mass produce nuclear fission power plants (to provide cheap and abundant nuclear power as the new primary source of baseload electricity).

- A crash program to commercialize fusion power (ensuring growing energy needs can be met long into the foreseeable future).

President Trump's call for "hundreds and hundreds of power plants" is right on track, as the perspective

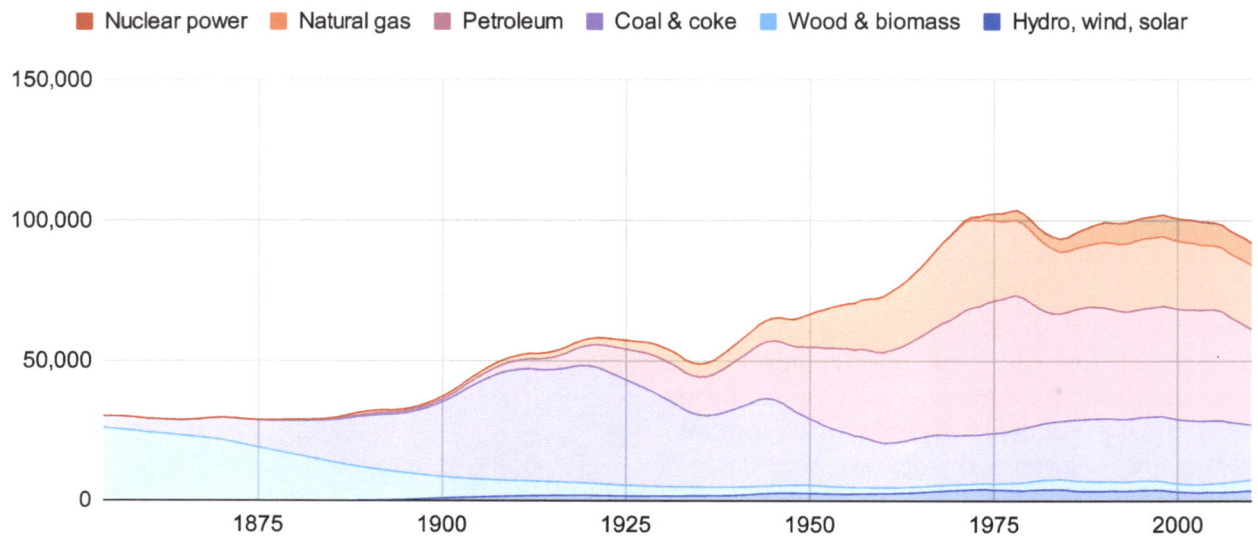

USA Primary Energy Consumption per Capita (kWh/yr)

US Energy Information Administration (Aug 2020), US Census Bureau. Benjamin Deniston, 2020 (five year rolling average).

outlined above will require something in the range of 700 to 1,000 new large electric power plants.

The overall intended impact is to increase the availability and quality of energy throughout the economy, while substantially lowering the costs.

This will have nonlinear impacts and direct implications for a productive economy, as processes that are too energy-intensive today will become economical, easy, and regular practice after such an upshift. As discussed above, desalination on massive scales can address water needs on the West Coast, lower quality minerals and ores can be processed, and more energy intensive modes of production can be utilized to increase productivity. Again, this is where American System policies of public credit become key to ensuring we can make these investments in negentropic growth.

A competent infrastructure program today starts with large-scale projects for high-speed rail, new freshwater supplies, and major increases in energy supplies as an integrated perspective. This will create the basis for new economic growth through new cities, new manufacturing, new agriculture, and countless new commercial enterprises, while also increasing the productivity and efficiency of existing economic activities. A public credit system allows us to make these investments.

As we work to accomplish this upshifting of the entire territory of the United States, we also look to the initial development of infrastructure systems economically connecting the Earth, Moon, and Mars, as we expand out into the Solar System. This represents a profound expression of mankind's unique position in the universe. Despite the rantings of radical environmentalists and ivory tower academics, mankind is not just another animal species with a slightly bigger brain. Mankind is the only form of life that willfully reshapes and improves the surrounding environment. The entire history of human progress and development centers around this reality, and to suppress this activity (like the radical environmentalists have desired to do) is nothing less than evil – they are denying generations the ability to participate in a core part of what makes us human: the ability to create new and better conditions of life for future generations.

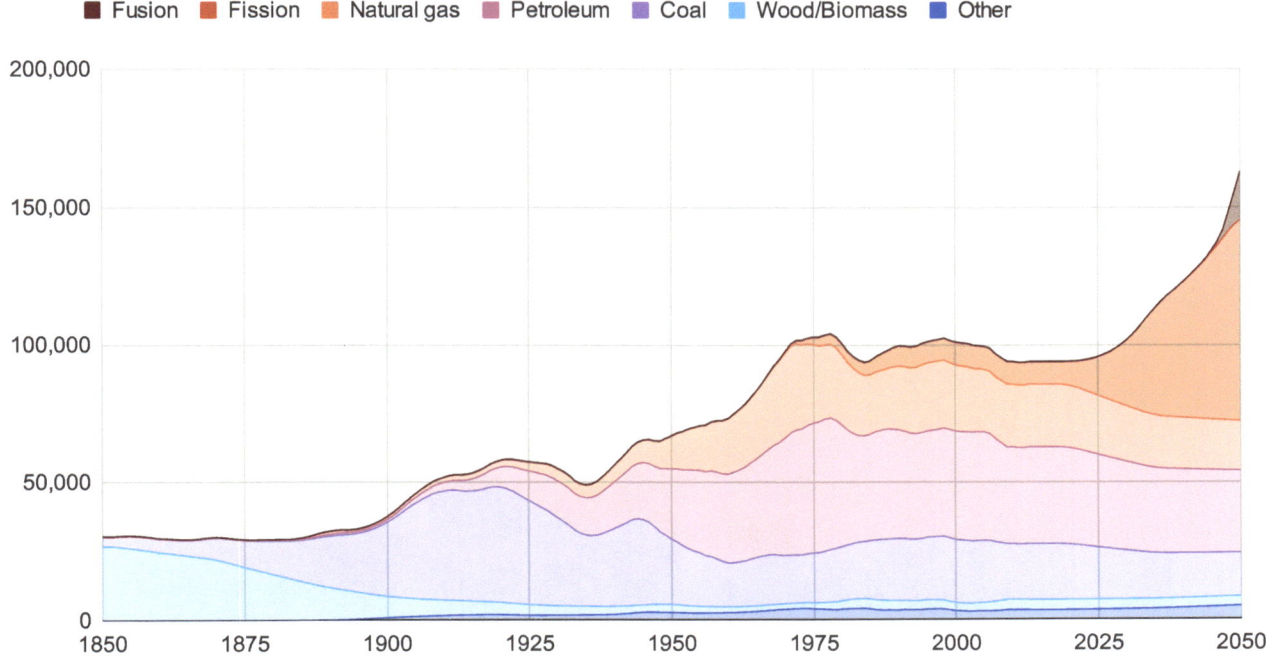

Growth Program: USA Primary Energy Consumption per Capita (kWh/yr)

US Energy Information Administration (Aug 2020), US Census Bureau. Benjamin Deniston, 2020 (five year rolling average).

Green Energy Is an Inflationary Boondoggle

Stripping away subsidies and other attempts to artificially lower the costs of wind and solar, we get a much clearer understanding of so-called green energy when we look at the physical costs for these systems in terms of their raw material requirements. Because wind and sunlight are inherently low density sources of energy, they require much larger amounts of land to capture enough energy. *Wind and solar require 300 to 400 times more land area compared with nuclear power to provide the same electricity.* This much larger land area has to be covered with vast arrays of wind turbines and solar panels, which require massive amounts of materials to produce. For a fair comparison, we can look at the raw materials required to build and maintain different electricity generation systems and compare that with the total energy they provide during their lifecycle. This allows us to compare the difference in the amount of steel, copper, concrete, etc. required to produce the same amount of electricity. The result? *Wind and solar require 10 to 15 times the raw materials to produce the same electricity as coal, natural gas, or nuclear power.* Thus the "Green New Deal" is inherently entropic (and hyperinflationary), since it needs vastly higher energy-of-the-system requirements (in raw material inputs, along with the labor required to produce those raw materials) to provide the same electricity output. *Simply put, you're dramatically increasing your costs, just to get the same product in the end, the perfect policy to destroy the economy.*

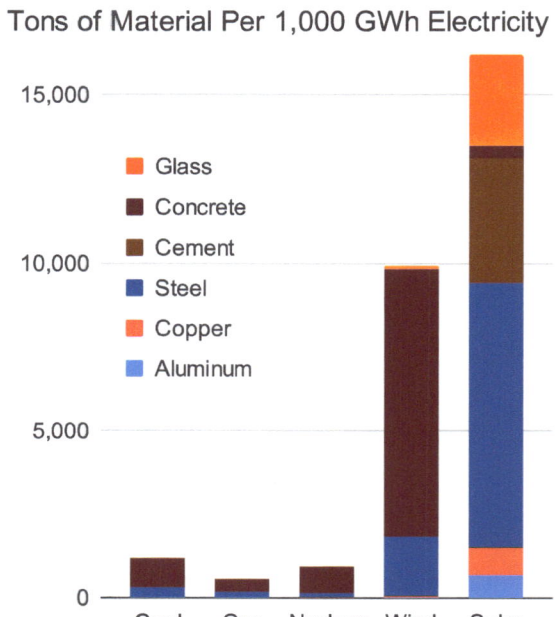

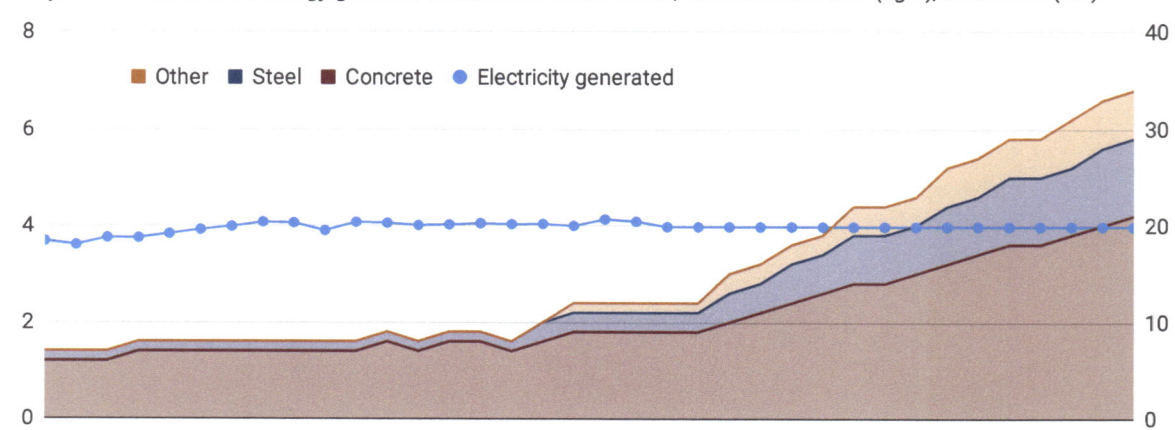

Nuclear Power Is Negentropic Growth

Throughout history, progress always comes with increasing energy throughput in the economy. A major factor enabling this type of progress has been the transitions to energy sources with higher and higher energy densities. The general progression has been from wood and biomass, to coal and coke, to oil, to natural gas, and on to uranium and thorium for nuclear fission, with hydrogen for nuclear fusion next on the horizon. As illustrated in the table, with each of these steps, less and less fuel is required to provide the same amount of energy.

Fuel Source	Weight / Equivalent	Energy Density (kWh / kg)
Wood	300 pounds	5
Coal	200 pounds	7.5
Diesel gasoline	16 gallon gas tank	13
Natural Gas	90 pounds	15
Typical fission fuel	A paperclip	1,000,000
Deuterium-Tritium fusion	A grain of rice	90,000,000

Following this progression ensures negentropic growth, as increasing energy supplies can be provided with the same, or even lower, energy-of-the-system requirements. For example, a 25-year program to increase electricity generation by expanding nuclear power and phasing out wind and solar could double total electricity generation with essentially no change in the required raw material inputs.

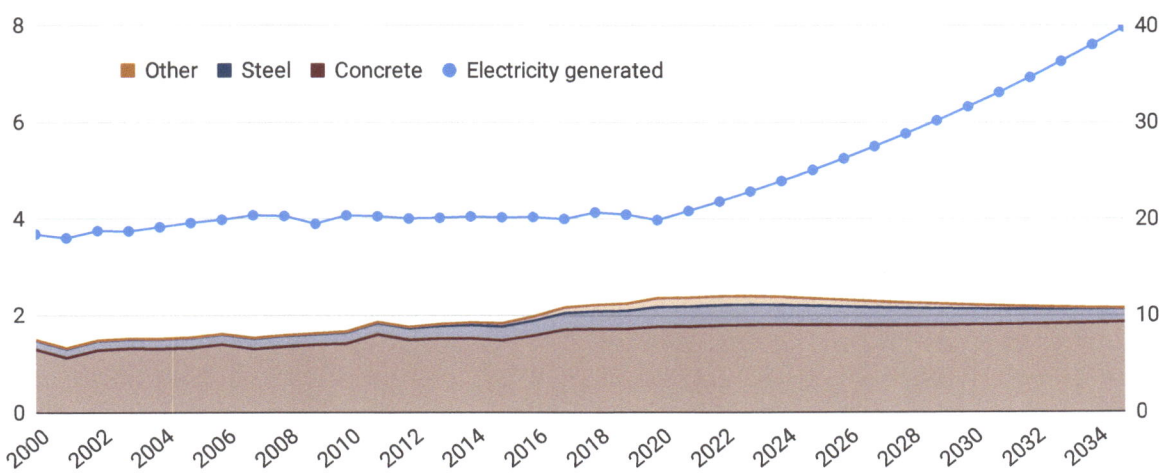

Promethean Action Nuclear Plan • Annual Electricity vs Material Inputs
Benjamin Deniston, 2021. Energy.gov 2015-Quadrennial Tech Review, US EIA. Million tons (right), trillion kWh (left).

Part 3 — On The Significance of Space and Fusion

Mankind's True Place in the Universe

This is a condensed version of a longer article available at www.Prom.ac/EFD

Today, we are on the verge of a transformation unlike any before in human history. The development of fusion power represents an essentially limitless energy source for mankind, while the colonization of space represents our expansion into an essentially limitless frontier. Taken together, these represent an unparalleled upshift in the significance and capabilities of mankind's position in the universe.

With fusion power, we're capturing the energy released from the combining of the lightest elements in the periodic table. These fuel sources for fusion power are orders of magnitude more abundant than fossil fuels or fuels for nuclear fission power, and the energy density of fusion reactions is hard to wrap one's head around. Fusion power fuels provide roughly a million times more energy per weight, when compared with fossil fuels, meaning it would only take a few grams of fusion fuel to provide the electricity needs of an American citizen for an entire year. *Simply incredible!* While government funding for fusion research has been far too limited, in recent years, various private ventures have started making significant progress in cracking the challenges of controlled fusion power.

At the same time, we have the technologies to begin the process of human colonization and development of the Solar System. The Moon and Mars represent the first targets, where we could set up initial outposts, and learn how to develop and utilize the resources available in these locations. Interest is already growing for expanded commercial activities in space, including mining resources available in asteroids and other bodies in the Solar System. Once we begin to develop the capabilities to manufacture goods in space, utilizing the resources available in space, we've freed ourselves from the expensive bottleneck of needing to lift everything required off the surface of Earth, and we've initiated an interplanetary economy. Fusion power will then play a critical role as well, not only providing electrical power, but being the only fuel source with the energy densities that can enable rapid transport around the Solar System.

These breakthroughs are awaiting us, but few seem to understand their true significance. The core problem stems from the deep corruption and degeneration in our educational system, scientific institutions, and in our culture. People no longer understand the importance and significance of mankind's place in the universe. People no longer celebrate the beauty of human progress.

Today, it has become almost routine for young children to be taught in our schools that the human species is a cancer on the planet, that we are murdering "Mother Earth." Corrupt scientific institutions proclaim the "consensus" that mankind is nothing more than another animal species, with life itself being nothing more than a temporary, random occurrence in a Godless universe that is ultimately heading toward an entropic heat death, in which any and all actions you take during your life are meaningless. For generations, the dignity of man has been under this fierce oligarchical attack. So to understand the true significance of fusion power and space colonization, we have to reassess what we know about the universe and man's place therein.

Our Creative & Developing Universe

We have a specific metric that allows us to examine the development of the entire universe and the activities of mankind in one coherent picture: energy flux-density. Originally developed by Lyndon LaRouche for studying physical economics, in the most general sense, energy flux-density is the measure of the energy functionally used by a system or process, per time, per constituent part.[1] This gives us an excellent measure of the level of development and complexity of a system.[2]

Utilizing this simple metric, we can measure the development of stars and galaxies, the evolution of life and the biosphere, and the development of human society all on one scale. These are the core, evolving systems that determine the overall complexity and potential of the universe, and, when comparing apples to apples, our universal metric of energy flux-density clearly shows mankind as the most powerful creative force in a creative universe. This revelation should become the basis for rejecting the present "scientific consensus" on mankind's position in the universe, and developing a culture that embraces and celebrates the beauty of human progress.

Start by examining the evolution and development of entire galaxies and individual stars. For galaxies, the evolution, from the earliest stages of formation to a well-formed galaxy like our own, will be measured by about a 50-fold increase in energy flux-density. However, this is mostly determined by the stars that compose the galaxies and individual stars operate at energy flux-densities at least 50 times higher than galaxies.[3] For a typical star, from its initial formation stage to the end stages of its lifecycle, its development is measured by about a 100-fold increase in energy flux-density.

This development is powered by stellar nuclear fusion, which is responsible for the generation of the full periodic table — the oxygen you're breathing now, the carbon in your body, the iron in your blood, all this was produced by stars through fusion. The development of the full periodic table of over 90 elements (and over 300 isotopes) from only a few initial starting elements can be thought of as a negentropic process, creating more organized states, with higher complexity and greater potential. Thus, as the stars go through their lifecycle, they act as negentropic agents, shaping and advancing the material and energetic characteristics of galaxies.

As with stars and the galaxies they define, the development of life over evolutionary time is also measured by increasing energy flux-density. Further, like stars, living organisms act as negentropic agents, creating and increasing the negentropy in their sphere of influence, defining the biosphere. Taking amphibians as representative of life 350 million years ago, we start out at an energy flux-density 7 times higher than a fully-developed star.[4] Next, we look to reptiles as representative of the age of the dinosaurs (from 250 to 65 million years ago), with energy flux-densities twice that of amphibians. And today's mammals are 30 times the energy flux-density of reptiles.

How Mankind Is Special

This takes us to mankind and the physical economy. Starting at the origins of mankind, if we hypothesize a purely biological existence, the energy flux-density for mankind is essentially the same as for other mammal species. However, since the beginnings of mankind's use of fire, we see the human species depart from merely a biological mode of existence, and begin building an existence dependent upon forms of energy flux-density that are created and controlled through human cognition.

At an agricultural stage of development, the energy flux-density of the physical economy is four times a mammalian biological existence. An industrial society is three times higher than an agricultural, and a technological society is three times that of an industrial. We gain greater insights when we focus on the primary fuel sourc-

---

1. This can be per mass, volume, area, or person, depending on the process or system you're measuring.
2. This section utilizes data from the following sources: Chaisson, Eric J. 2014. "The Natural Science Underlying Big History," doi:10.1155/2014/384912; Hoehler, "The metabolic rate of the biosphere and its components," *PNAS* Vol. 120, No. 25, 6/12/23; Seaborg, Glenn, 1962, "Civilian Nuclear Power—A Report to the President," U.S. AEC; U.S. Energy Information Agency's "Annual Energy Review 2011; "AnAge: The Animal Ageing and Longevity Database," http://genomics.senescence.info/species.
3. Remember, we're measuring per unit mass, so, even though a galaxy is obviously more energetic in absolute terms, per unit mass, stars are more powerful.

4. Obviously, a star is far more energetic in absolute terms, but not per unit mass.

es powering a physical economy. Taking the history of the United States as an example, going from the peak of a wood-powered economy (in the early 1800s) to the peak of a coal-powered economy (in the early 1900s) corresponded to a doubling of the energy flux-density of the U.S. economy. The transition from coal to the peak of an oil-and-gas-powered economy (in the 1970s) nearly doubled the value again, while nuclear fission and fusion power promise further leaps we haven't come close to realizing yet.

Thus, with mankind, we have a new negentropic agent, acting to generate the highest levels of energy flux-density that we observe in the universe (in terms of the developing systems that determine the complexity of the universe), objectively and empirically placing mankind at the pinnacle of a creative and developing universe. How has mankind been able to do this? A profound insight comes from the ancient Greek legend of Prometheus, who freed mankind from the tyranny of the oligarchical gods who sought to suppress humanity by denying them access to their own creativity. If we look back to Aeschylus's telling of this legend in *Prometheus Bound*, Prometheus brings all forms of knowledge to mankind: astronomy, cooking, arts, agriculture, and so on. But, the legend of Prometheus centers around one specific act—the stealing of fire from the gods—and, across thousands of years, Prometheus remains known as the fire-bringer.

In the context of our unified scientific picture of the universe, what is the significance of fire under the control and use by mankind? It is the first expression of a negentropic agent managing an external energy flux-density to expand its capabilities to transform and expand its sphere of influence. We can look back to the mastery of fire to accomplish tasks that improve the conditions of life—providing warmth, cooking food, and enabling improvements in tool-making. These are activities that changed mankind's ability to exist, activities that changed mankind's relation to the natural world.

Rather than our relation to the natural world being solely mediated by our biology and instincts (as with the animals), we see the emergence of the superior mediating factor of human creativity. But, for human creativity to be expressed and sustained through society, requires a level of fire (energy flux-density), supporting a unique and new form of material and energetic relation with the natural world, called physical economy. From the manufacturing of goods, to

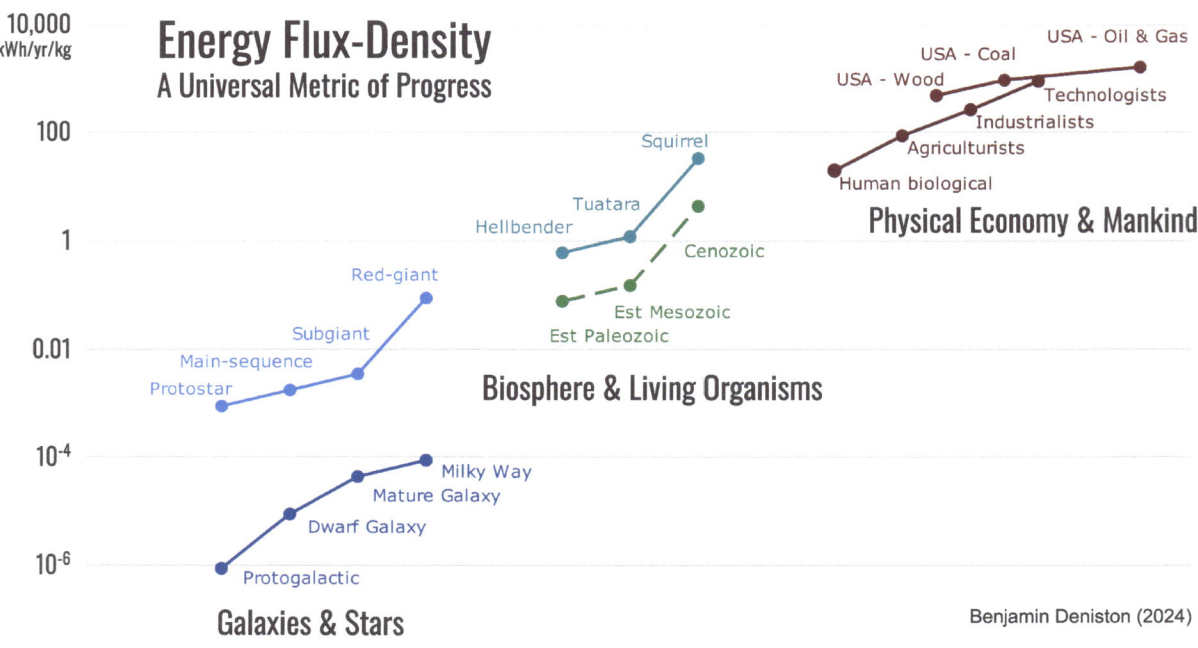

the agricultural work that feeds society, to the construction of the infrastructure that society runs on, the physical processes that are required to sustain society require a minimum level of energy flux-density to maintain.

Thus, physical economy has a profound meaning as a regime of negentropy that is the expression of human creativity, and provides concrete proof of mankind's distinction from the animals. The very nature, existence, and definition of mankind centers around changing the natural world, and bringing increasing levels of the natural world under the domain of mankind's negentropic sphere of influence. Only when you understand this can you truly understand why a public credit system works.

Why Mankind Is Special

Human creativity, as manifested in the form of physical economy, appears as a sort of inversion in the nested process of creative development of the universe. This process goes from the evolution of galaxies and stars, to the evolution of life and the biosphere, to mankind and physical economy. But the evolution of the physical economy is different. The increasing energy flux-density of galaxies is driven by the development of stars. The increasing energy flux-density of the biosphere is driven by the evolution of life. But the increasing energy flux-density of the physical economy is not driven by changes in the physical expression of mankind. Instead mankind discovers and manages external energy flux-densities which are the products of these more fundamental systems, starting with successive levels of energy flux-density of life and the biosphere, followed by levels of energy flux-density of stars and galaxies.

At an earlier stage, human society was dependent on burning wood and other biomass. That fuel source was the product of the biosphere in real time, and enabled a physical economy capable of being the peak formation of life in the biosphere (roughly corresponding to an agricultural stage of development).

The current stage of human society is approaching the peak of a fossil-fuel-powered economy. That is a physical economy powered by the products of the biosphere over evolutionary time: fossil fuels. At this level, the physical economy is capable of generating negentropic actions only otherwise seen by biospheric activity over evolutionary time. For example,

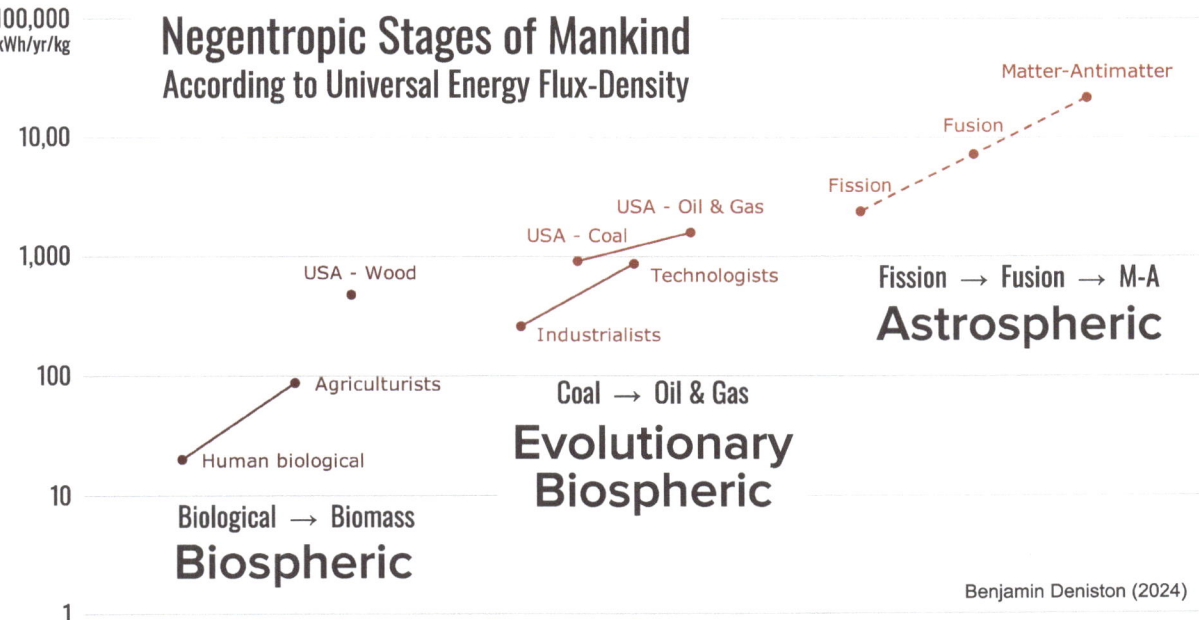

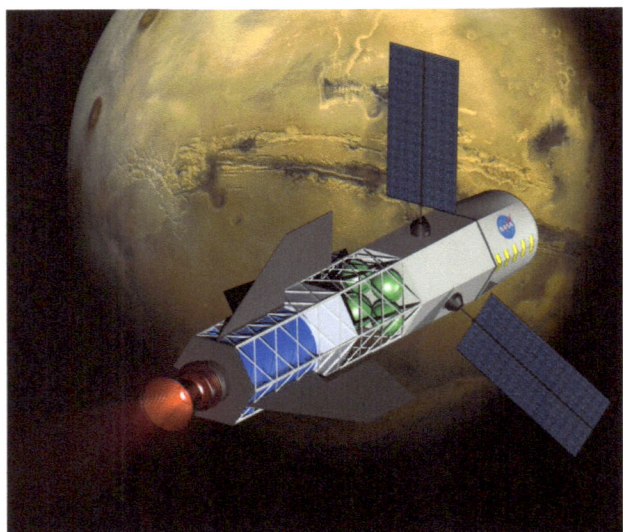

Fusion rocket. Credit: Pancotti, U of Washington, MSNW.

over the last couple thousand years, mankind has doubled the energy flux-density of the biosphere, a change only otherwise seen over the evolutionary development of life over millions of years. Stated another way, if you only looked at the energy flux-density impact of mankind's actions on the biosphere, it would look like the product of evolutionary improvement of life over millions of years. Yet mankind has generated this change on the scale of merely thousands of years, and done so via a fossil-fueled physical economy, rather than biological evolution.

With both the fuel source powering the physical economy and the impact of mankind's actions measured in terms of biospheric evolutionary timescales, *a fossil-fuel-powered physical economy represents mankind as an evolutionary biospheric force.* And the next great stage of human development is clear. Is it a coincidence that the current frontiers of the physical economy encapsulate both nuclear power and colonization of the solar system? As fossil fuels are products of the biosphere over evolutionary time, fission and fusion fuels are the products of stellar processes over successive generations of stars over stellar and galactic time. As a fully-developed fossil-fuel-powered physical economy is the representation of mankind as an evolutionary biospheric force, a fully-developed nuclear-fusion-powered physical economy will be the representation of mankind as an "astrospheric" force, capable of bringing the solar system (and other stellar systems) under his regime of negentropic control.

Thus, the frontiers of fusion power and space colonization represent the coming transition of mankind from a biospheric evolutionary force into the very beginnings of an astrospheric force. A profound change that illustrates mankind's special place in the universe and the basis to design today's American System 2.0 policies.

We live in a universe composed of nested processes of creative development, characterized by systems of increasing complexity and potential generated by the actions of negentropic agents. Within that process, mankind is a unique negentropic agent, expressing a power we call human creativity. But human creativity and science aren't just about understanding random facts about the natural world. Human creativity has a specific expression, the expansion of the sphere of mankind's negentropic impact over increasingly larger domains, and more fundamental systems composing the developmental process of the universe itself. That is, mankind encapsulating, expressing, and representing the creative systems that compose the universe in increasingly more fundamental and powerful ways. That is a scientific expression and definition for mankind in the image of God, the basis to develop a culture that embraces and celebrates the beauty of mankind as a creative force, and the reason the American System worked before, and will work again as the American System 2.0.

Join our campaign for The American System 2.0

A growing coalition of Americans is fighting for economic growth through a revival of the American System of Economics.

Prom.ac/AmSys2

www.ingramcontent.com/pod-product-compliance
Lightning Source LLC
Chambersburg PA
CBHW042020150426
43197CB00002B/84